WHO IN THE WORLD WAS THE FORGOTTEN EXPLORER?

THE STORY OF AMERIGO VESPUCCI

by Lorene Lambert
Illustrations by Jed Mickle

 Peace Hill Press
Charles City, VA

Books for the Well-Trained Mind

Publisher's Cataloging-in-Publication Data

Lambert, Lorene.

Who in the world was the forgotten explorer? : the story of
Amerigo Vespucci / by Lorene Lambert ; illustrations by Jed Mickle.
p. : ill., map ; cm. — (Who in the world)
Includes index.

SUMMARY:

Covers the life of Amerigo Vespucci, from his boyhood
in Florence to his days as an explorer for Spain and
Portugal.

Audience: Ages 5-12.

LCCN 2005906405
ISBN 0-9728603-8-X

1. Vespucci, Amerigo, 1451–1512 — Juvenile literature.
2. Explorers — America — Biography — Juvenile literature.
3. Explorers — Spain — Biography — Juvenile literature.
4. Explorers — Portugal — Biography — Juvenile literature.
5. America — Discovery and exploration — Spanish — Juvenile literature.
6. America — Discovery and exploration — Portugese — Juvenile literature.
7. Vespucci, Amerigo, 1451–1512.   8. Explorers.
9. America — Discovery and exploration — Spanish.
10. America — Discovery and exploration — Portugese.

I. Mickle, Jed.
II. Title.
III. Title: Forgotten explorer.

E125.V5 L36 2005   970.01/6/092
2005906405

**This *Who in the World* reader complements *The Story of the World, Vol. 2:
The Middle Ages* (ISBN 978-1-933339-09-2), also published by Peace Hill Press.**

Peace Hill Press is an independent publisher creating high-quality educational books.
Our award-winning resources—in history, reading, and grammar—are used by parents,
teachers, libraries, and schools that want their students to be passionate about learning.
For more about us, please visit our website, www.peacehillpress.com.

Table of Contents

Amerigo leaned out from his window,
tipping his head back to look at the stars.

CHAPTER 1

A NEW ROUTE TO THE INDIES

Hundreds of years ago, the great Italian city of Florence was very dark at night. No streetlamps or billboards cast up their glow. No floodlights shone down on baseball fields. When the sky grew dusky, the streets filled with shadows and the bustling city noises disappeared. The river Arno reflected the stars overhead as it flowed past the lamplit houses.

In a mansion close to the river, a boy named Amerigo leaned out from his window, tipping his head back to look at the stars. He loved the night sky. His uncle Giorgio had taught him to see the patterns that the stars made, the constellations. Uncle Giorgio showed Amerigo how they moved and wheeled through the sky as the seasons changed.

He told Amerigo how the sailors in their ships far out on the Ocean Sea could use the stars to steer toward land.

"Amerigo?" His uncle's voice called.

He pulled his head back through the window, and looked across the room to the table where Uncle Giorgio sat. A large map was spread before him, in the pool of light made by a flickering candle. He beckoned Amerigo to his side.

"Look at this," he said. "What do you see?"

Amerigo walked over and leaned his elbows on the table, studying the map. It was like many others he had looked at. There were three large areas of land, which were the continents of Europe, Asia, and Africa, with the Ocean Sea surrounding them like a large blue band. But in most maps, the Sea was filled with drawings of fantastic beasts, half man and half fish. This map had no drawings. There were only pictures of the land and the sea, with long straight lines going up, down and across. The lines divided the whole paper into little squares.

"Do you remember Paolo Toscanelli?" asked Uncle Giorgio.

Amerigo nodded. Signor Toscanelli was an old friend of the Vespucci family. He was a physician and a cosmographer, which means someone who studies the stars and planets. He explored far-away lands just by thinking about them. And he was famous for the beautiful maps that he drew.

Uncle Giorgio tapped the map with the knuckles of one fist and said, "He made this."

Uncle Giorgio tapped the map with the knuckles of one fist and said, "He made this."

3

Amerigo peered down at it. "It looks different, from other maps," he said. Slowly he traced his finger along one of the long lines from the right side of the paper to the left, east to west. His finger stopped on a picture of a group of islands, some large and some tiny. "What place is this, Uncle?"

Uncle Giorgio chuckled. "Ah, my boy, you've put your finger on the Indies. Dr. Toscanelli believes you may reach the Indies faster by sailing to the West." He touched the left side of the map.

"But, how can that be?" Amerigo was puzzled. The Indies were those lands far, far to the east, in Asia, places called China and India and all the islands around them. Wonderful things came from the Indies. Amerigo had seen them in the market, piles of bright spices, rolls of shining silk cloth, and cunningly carved boxes made of sweet-smelling woods.

Amerigo knew that getting from Europe to the Indies was very difficult. Those lands could only be reached by a long journey over land to the east, on a pathway called the Silk Road. Much of that journey passed through countryside ruled by the fierce Turks, who hated Europeans. Some people thought that maybe you could get around the Turks by sailing up to the north or down to the south. But the way north was blocked with ice, and you could not sail south beyond Africa, either, because the Equator was there. Amerigo shivered. Everyone knew that the Equator was dangerous! He himself had heard Paolo Toscanelli say that the ancient Greeks and

Romans thought the Equator was a ring of fire! Anyone who sailed there would be blasted by flames shooting down from the sky!

But now Dr. Toscanelli had drawn a map showing the Indies on the far left side instead of on the right. Amerigo stared at the map, and then looked up at his uncle. "How can you go east by sailing west? I don't understand."

Uncle Giorgio reached over to a basket of fruit that sat in the middle of the table, and picked up an apple. "Well, you know that the world is round, like this apple." Uncle Giorgio pulled a small knife from his pocket and carved a large X in its skin. "Let's pretend that this is the Indies, right here."

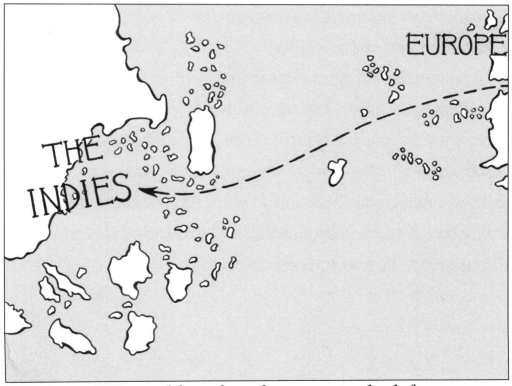

"We could go the other way, to the left,
and still come to the Indies."

Then he made another, tiny X on the other side of the apple, and showed it to Amerigo. "And this is us, here in Florence. Do you understand so far?"

Amerigo nodded. Uncle Giorgio held up the apple, and put his finger on the little X that represented Florence.

"Now, we can get to the Indies by going east" he said, "like this." And he moved his finger to the right along the apple's skin until he came to the big X. "Or, we could go the other way, to the left, and still come to the Indies." He moved his finger back to the tiny X and then went to the left, all the way around the apple to the large X that showed the Indies.

Amerigo was nodding vigorously. "I see it, Uncle! But, surely that's a very long way to sail?"

"Toscanelli thinks not. He thinks it would be much shorter to sail west to the Indies than to travel over the Silk Road."

His uncle carefully rolled up the map, and then sent Amerigo off to bed. As he lay in the darkness, watching the starlight make shadows on the wall, Amerigo thought about that map. And he remembered to say a prayer of gratitude that he was allowed to study such things.

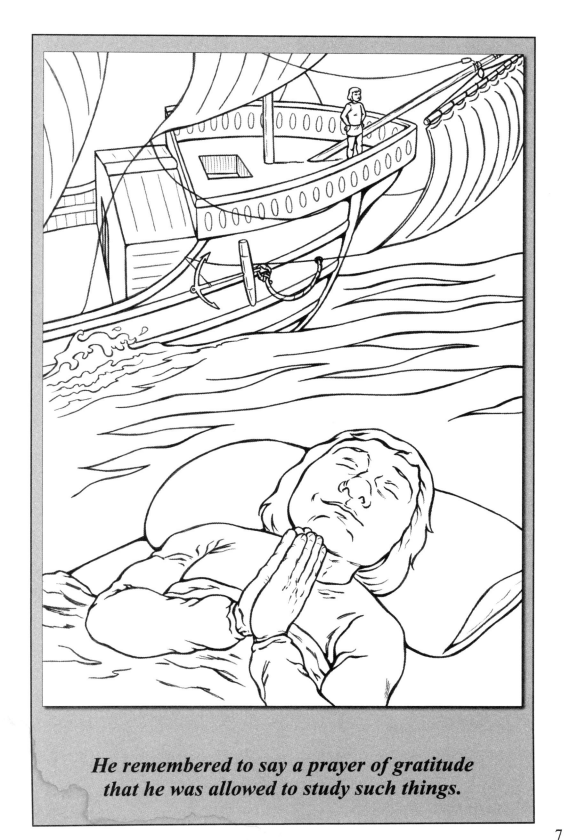

*He remembered to say a prayer of gratitude
that he was allowed to study such things.*

CHAPTER 2

A THIRD SON

Amerigo knew he was a very lucky boy.

He was a third son. In our times, that would only mean that he had two brothers who were older than he, but in those days, a third son could usually expect a hard life. He would not be able to inherit any of his father's money, lands or power, because all of those things would be given to the first son. The second son might be given a little money to go to school and learn to be a lawyer or a philosopher. But the third son was almost always expected to begin working hard, as soon as he was old enough to read and write.

Amerigo, however, belonged to a powerful family. His father was Anastagio Vespucci, and the Vespucci family was

He had a wonderful library, filled
to the topmost shelf with books about Latin,
mathematics, astronomy and literature.

rich and well known in Florence. They were good friends with the Medici family, who ruled the entire city.

Because of his wealth and power, Anastagio Vespucci was able to give his third son Amerigo a special opportunity. Instead of having to go to work after he learned to read and write, Amerigo had been sent to live with his uncle. Uncle Giorgio was a famous teacher, with many students from all over Italy and Europe. He had a wonderful library, filled to the topmost shelf with books about Latin, mathematics, astronomy and literature. He collected maps of every sort, and he taught Amerigo all that he knew about these things. Amerigo wrote about what he was learning in a little notebook that he kept close by him. In it he wrote, "I want to do something to win fame and honor!"

Amerigo lived in his uncle's house and learned all that he could. He loved the maps, and even started his own collection. He did not forget about the Indies, and the problem of reaching them. He thought a lot about Dr. Toscanelli's map.

Then, when he was nineteen years old, he heard exciting news. Sailors from a country west of Italy called Portugal had crossed the Equator. And they were not burned up! No ring of fire stretched up in a solid wall to block their way. No greedy flames reached out to seize and devour their ships. Carefully following the sandy coastline, they could go all the way around the tip of Africa, and then, perhaps, on to the Indies. They would reach the east by sailing south!

"Wonderful news, indeed," Amerigo thought. How amazing to be one of those sailors, seeing those far coasts for the first time! He wished he had been a part of that voyage. And he thought, "Perhaps now no one will try to go west to reach the east."

For the next few years, the Portuguese sailors continued to explore farther and farther down the coast of Africa. Amerigo remained with Uncle Giorgio, studying diligently every day. By the time he was twenty-four, he had filled many notebooks with his writings, and finished his studies. Uncle Giorgio praised him highly and his family boasted about his fine education, but Amerigo felt a little sad when he returned to his father's house. He wondered, "Now, what will I do?"

One day, as he sat in the courtyard of his father's fine house, the deep bong of the bell at the entrance gate interrupted his thoughts, and a few minutes later a servant hurried toward him. "Signor, you must go at once to your uncle Guido Vespucci. He has need of you."

This was an unexpected summons. Uncle Guido had servants and employees to do his bidding. What could he possibly want with Amerigo?

He hurried to his uncle's house, and found him in the stable at the back, carefully inspecting a riding horse while a servant held the bridle.

"Ah, Amerigo! Thank you for coming so quickly."

"How can I help you, Uncle?" Amerigo asked politely.

Uncle Guido nodded at the servant, who walked the horse away, and turned to Amerigo. "Our ruler Lorenzo de Medici is sending me to the city of Paris, in France, to be his ambassador to the King there, and to do some trading for him. Would you like to come along as my assistant?"

Amerigo grinned. "Of course, Uncle! You did not even need to ask."

Uncle Guido clapped him on the shoulder. "Then you'd better pack your things. We leave soon!"

Paris was far from Florence, so Amerigo and his uncle passed through many other lands and cities as they journeyed. In every city, Uncle Guido stopped and lingered, trading spices for sheep's wool, and sheep's wool for cedar wood. He came away from every trade with more and more money for the Medici family, because he always traded the things he had for things that were even more valuable. Amerigo watched and learned. He learned to bargain for the best price, and to sell things in large quantities. He learned how to tell if a merchant was honest, what months of the year to buy woolen cloth, and when spices went stale and lost their value. By the time they had finished their business in Paris and traveled back to Florence, two whole years had passed. Amerigo was twenty-six years old.

But sadness came to the Vespucci family soon after Amerigo returned. Anastagio Vespucci, Amerigo's well-

In every city, Uncle Guido stopped and lingered, trading spices for sheep's wool, and sheep's wool for cedar wood.

loved father, died. After they had mourned for him, and Amerigo's oldest brother became head of the family, Amerigo was unsure about his future. He was the third son, and now his father, who had given him so much, was gone. His journey with Uncle Guido was over. What would he do now?

Fortunately, though, Amerigo had done well as assistant to his uncle, and Lorenzo de Medici, the ruler of Florence, had noticed. Soon after Anastagio's death, Lorenzo sent a message to Amerigo, asking him if he would like to oversee a bank in Spain for the Medici family. Just like that, Amerigo became a banker.

CHAPTER 3

WORKING FOR COLUMBUS

The Medici family wanted Amerigo to travel to the city of Seville, in Spain, to take charge of the bank there. Also, they instructed Amerigo to find a man named Gianetto Berardi and become partners with him. Berardi and Amerigo would work together to build a ship-supplying business. They would help ships get ready to sail to far-away places.

Seville was a wonderful city! Amerigo loved its white, curvy buildings, so different from Florence, and its huge markets with spices and fruits, silk and wool, and treasures from all over the world. The food and music in the restaurants were different, too, but he tried all the new foods, and tapped his fingers as the tambourines jingled. He was very happy, even though he had to learn a new language.

Seville was a wonderful city!

Amerigo arrived in Seville in the year 1492. Since the beginning of that year, all of Seville had been abuzz with news of a man named Christopher Columbus. Columbus, it seemed, did not think that sailing around the tip of Africa was a good way to reach the Indies. He insisted that he could find a better way, a faster way, by sailing west across the Ocean Sea! And to show that what he was saying was true, he was carrying a map made by Paolo Toscanelli, a special map with long straight lines that divided it into little squares.

Toscanelli's map! Amerigo himself had studied a copy of that same map all those years ago in his Uncle Giorgio's library. Amerigo told his business partner Berardi that Toscanelli was a great mapmaker and scholar.

"Perhaps this Columbus is not so crazy, then," said Berardi.

"So he's actually going then?" Amerigo asked. "He will sail to the Indies by going west?"

"That's what he says."

Amerigo and Berardi became friends with Christopher Columbus. He stayed often at Berardi's house, talking about his planned voyage, and his methods of finding his way across the dark Ocean Sea. He was certain that he would discover the Indies by sailing west across the globe, because as far as he knew there was nothing but ocean between the coasts of Europe and the spice-scented beaches of the Indies. He had much work to do to get ready for such a long trip. He needed at least three ships, and many barrels of supplies.

Finally, late in the summer of that year, he sent a message to Amerigo and Berardi. "I am leaving at last!"

And so, one day in August, in the year 1492, Columbus sailed away from a small town on the sea, near Seville. Amerigo and Berardi watched from the shore as the three little ships grew smaller and smaller until they disappeared from sight. Amerigo sighed. He would have liked to have gone along.

Slowly, the weeks and months passed, and, when Columbus did not come back, whispers began to fill the city. He was lost! The ships were sunk! He would never return! By the seventh month, even Berardi and Amerigo were wondering if they would ever see Columbus again.

Then, suddenly, the news reached Seville that Columbus's ships had been sighted on the horizon. One of his ships had wrecked, but he had sailed back to Spain with the two others, and, best of all, he had found the Indies. He had discovered some lovely islands, with blowing palm trees and sandy beaches.

In our day, all children learn that Columbus discovered America in 1492, and this is true. The islands that he found were in the Caribbean Sea, south of the state of Florida. But Columbus did not know this. He was certain that those islands were just off the coast of China itself. He felt sure that it could only be a short distance further to India and the rest of Asia. He did not think for one moment that he had discovered something entirely new.

Amerigo was happy for his friend's success, especially when Columbus was called to the palace of the King and

He had discovered some lovely islands,
with blowing palm trees and sandy beaches.

Queen in the city of Barcelona. When he returned from seeing them, he came to visit his friends and told them his news while Amerigo rummaged out some bread and cheese for the three of them to dine on.

"I am made Admiral of the Open Sea," Columbus said, slapping the table in his excitement. "All the exploring of the Indies is now my responsibility. I must plan another voyage, at once!" He grinned at them. "And I wish the two of you to take charge of supplying my ships."

Amerigo and Berardi were pleased to help with the difficult job of getting the ships ready. Instead of three ships, Columbus was sailing west this time with seventeen. Amerigo sent servants scurrying like busy ants, back and forth across Seville, trying to trade for or buy every cask of honey and barrel of biscuits in the city. He tired out ten different horses as he rode from Seville to Barcelona and other cities, hurrying to gather all of the food, weapons, and money that Columbus needed. Soon wagonloads of supplies began winding their way through the city down to the docks, and the ships sank lower and lower in the water as their holds filled up with all the things that were needed for such a long, important voyage.

Columbus sailed away again in September of 1493, but Amerigo and Berardi were not able to rest. The king gave them the special job of supplying other ships that were sailing to these newfound islands. Amerigo was often down by the docks, a roll of parchment in his hand to keep track of the

*Berardi and Amerigo took charge
of supplying ships for the King.*

supplies that were loaded on the ships. He loved the briny smell of the ocean, and the sailors' stories of flying fish and huge waves and strange rocky islands.

Things did not go as well for Columbus this time. He could not seem to find India or China or any of the other parts of Asia. Some of his sailors grew impatient, and sent bad reports of him to the King and Queen. They said he was keeping treasure for himself, and treating the island people cruelly. The King listened to these reports with a stern face, and then gave a new edict. No longer was Columbus alone in charge of exploring the Indies. Any Spaniard who wanted to explore could go without having to report to him.

Amerigo and Berardi were sorry that their friend had not been successful. They decided to try for themselves. Perhaps they could find the way through these new islands to China or India. They began to buy and borrow sturdy ships, and gather barrels of food and fresh water for their own trip to the Indies.

And then, in the midst of all of their exciting plans, Berardi became sick, and he died. What a sad day for Amerigo! He and Berardi had worked together for many years, and had been good business partners. Amerigo continued his preparations, but his heart was heavy.

CHAPTER 4

A SUMMONS FROM THE KING

While preparing his ships, Amerigo received a message from the King himself. The King was unsure whether the bad reports about Columbus were true. He wanted to find out what was really happening, and he had set up a fleet of four ships, to leave in May of 1499. Would Amerigo be willing to give up his own plans, and sail instead on one of the King's ships, as the pilot?

This was a great honor. The pilot was in charge of making sure that the ship was on the right course. Amerigo sent a polite letter to the King, to tell him that he would be happy to serve as a pilot. Then, he began to pack his things and prepare to leave. He was going exploring!

He met the man who would be the captain of the four ships,

After all these years of studying maps, supplying ships and talking to sailors, Amerigo was a sailor himself!

Alonso de Ojeda, and impressed him with his knowledge of astronomy and maps. Captain de Ojeda told him, "I am pleased indeed to have such an educated man as one of my pilots."

"I have never actually sailed before," Amerigo said. "All I know is what I have learned from books and maps, and listening to sailors."

"That will be enough," said Captain de Ojeda.

Amerigo's steps were light with happiness as he boarded his ship on the morning of May 16, 1499. After all these years of studying maps, supplying ships and talking to sailors, Amerigo was a sailor himself! It was a brand new feeling for him, to watch the land slip away and feel the deep ocean swells beneath the deck at his feet. He watched Alonso de Ojeda carefully, to learn about being the captain of these large ships.

Finally, after many weeks, Captain de Ojeda announced that they were probably within a few days sailing of the new islands. He was not entirely sure, because in those days, sailors had no way to measure how far east or west they had sailed each day. His words made the crewmen happy. Soon they would have fresh meat to eat, and fresh water. Amerigo looked over the rail into the blue-green seawater. He was thinking about the Indies. Surely they must be very near to Asia, now.

Then, the Captain came and talked with him in a low voice. "Amerigo, you have been an excellent pilot, and I've seen how the sailors on your ship respect you and obey your orders. I have a special job that needs to be done, and I think that you're the right man to do it."

"What job is that, sir?" Amerigo asked.

"All the area further down to the south of here has never been explored. Perhaps that is where the rest of Asia is! Will you take two ships and turn south alone? Will you explore those unknown seas?"

Amerigo's heart leaped. "We will not fail you, sir. We are ready for our voyage of discovery!"

Captain de Ojeda's ships sailed off toward the new islands in the north. Amerigo was on his own. He turned his face

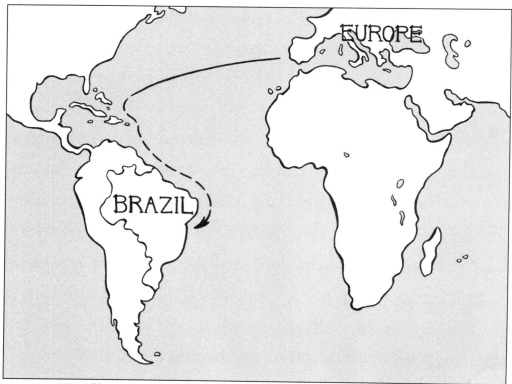

"Will you take two ships and turn south alone?
Will you explore those unknown seas?"

to the south, where no one from Europe had ever yet sailed. Strong, warm winds filled the sails of his ships and he raced along. On a lovely, windy morning in June, Amerigo and his men arrived at a green coast, where the jungle marched right out to the sea. Amerigo did not realize it yet, but he had discovered Brazil.

He directed the ships to keep sailing south, exploring the coastline as they went. Amerigo was amazed by what he was seeing. So many different kinds of trees, in a thousand shades of green, with delicious smells, and brightly colored birds winging from branch to branch. He saw an enormous snake, one afternoon, longer than his entire ship!

Amerigo sailed past the Equator, all the way down the coast of this huge new land. He discovered the mouth of a river bigger than any he had ever imagined—the Amazon River. Amerigo had not ever heard that the Indies had such huge rivers. He saw people with dark skin and clothing of bird feathers, who could shoot arrows at a tiny target and hit it. They didn't really look like Asian people to Amerigo, and he began to wonder. Was he really in Asia? Was this anywhere near the coast of China? At night, he would lie flat on the upper deck of his ship and study the stars, picking out bright constellations that he had never seen before. He had never been so happy.

While he was studying the strange new stars, Amerigo made an important discovery. He was looking at the moon

*He saw people with dark skin and
clothing of bird feathers, who could shoot arrows
at a tiny target and hit it.*

late one night as it rose over the horizon. As it moved, he saw that it was in a different place in the sky. Back home in Florence, he had made a chart that showed which planet the moon was near when it rose each night. But here, in this new tropical sky, the moon was rising near different planets and stars. Amerigo's brow furrowed as he thought about this. Slowly, he realized that, if he made a new chart showing which planet the moon was near as it rose, he could figure out how far west he had come. Amerigo's way of watching the moon became all sailors' way of knowing how far west they were for many, many years.

The long green coast kept going and going, stretching before them in an endless line. Amerigo wanted to keep following it, as far as he could. Surely the passage to Asia was there somewhere! But after several months, he had to turn back. His ships were being eaten by worms. If he kept going, his ships would sink. Amerigo and his men sailed back to Spain in the spring of the year 1500.

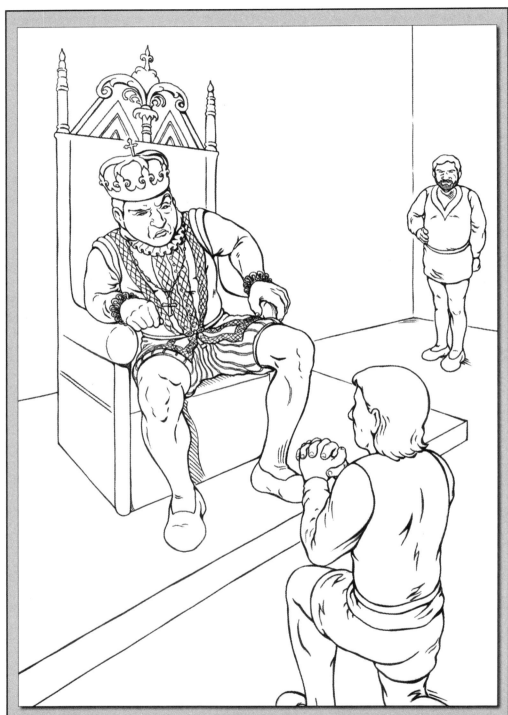

Amerigo pleaded with King Emmanuel of Portugal to let him go back to explore further, this time with Portuguese ships.

CHAPTER 5

THE FOURTH PART OF THE WORLD

Amerigo's mind was full of the fantastic things he had seen, and he was eager to explore further. But, when he went to the King and Queen of Spain, to ask their permission to go on another voyage, he received an unpleasant surprise. While he had been gone, the King of Spain and the King of Portugal had agreed that Portugal would do all the exploring of the southern lands that Amerigo had seen. Spanish ships would stay to the north.

Amerigo was determined to sail again. Off he went, to the city of Lisbon. There he pleaded with King Emmanuel of Portugal to let him go back, this time with Portuguese ships. In May of the year 1501, Amerigo sailed away from Lisbon as captain of a fleet of three ships. He was exploring again!

When he reached the new land, he sailed straight down the jungle coast until he started seeing places that no European had ever seen, countries that today we call Uruguay and Argentina. The strange coastline was almost barren in some spots, tangled and green in others, and the wind was always blowing. In fact, the weather grew so blustery, and the wind so cruel and cold, that at last Amerigo felt that he must turn back. If he had gone only a little farther, he would have reached the very tip of South America and sailed around into the Pacific Ocean, though of course he did not know that.

So Amerigo returned to Portugal, having been the successful captain of two voyages. But this time, when he came home to

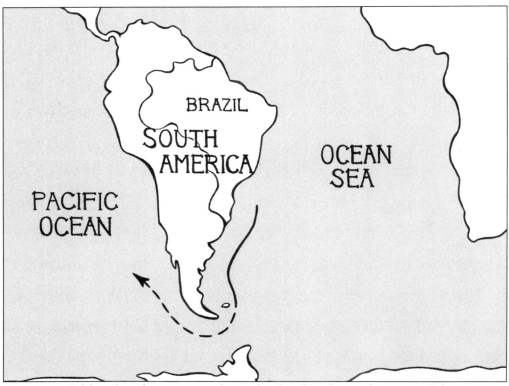

If he had gone only a little farther, he would have reached the very tip of South America.

Seville, his mind was full of something much more valuable than beautiful trees and birds and strange new coasts. He had an idea.

The coast along which he had sailed was too big, and its rivers too wide, he thought. It stretched too far south. It couldn't possibly be an island. And it couldn't possibly be China either. The people he had seen were certainly not Chinese. Amerigo was sure that he had discovered the reason that Columbus had not found China, India or any of the rest of the Indies. It was because China was still many, many miles away! What they had found was a new land, a new continent, completely separate from Europe, Asia and Africa. It was a fourth part of the world, to add to the other three, and Amerigo was the first one to realize this.

When he returned home, he sent a letter to the Medici family, the rulers of Florence. He often wrote to them and described his adventures and discoveries. In this letter, he excitedly told them his new idea.

"We arrived at a new land," he wrote, "which we observed to be a continent."

When people heard Amerigo's idea, they were amazed. The world was a much bigger place than most of them had ever dreamed. Now there were four continents, not just three, and the new continent was a whole New World, with miles and miles of jungles, mountains and deserts that no one had ever explored! Who knew what riches and wonders could be discovered there?

**When he returned home,
Amerigo sent a letter to the Medici family.**

Amerigo settled back into his life in Seville. He married a pretty Spanish lady named Maria, and he liked Spain so much he decided to become a citizen. The King of Spain was proud of Amerigo's discoveries, and was pleased by his news that Columbus had found, not the Indies, but a brand new continent. He wanted to reward Amerigo and put his sharp mind to good use. So he called Amerigo to the palace.

"Your Majesty," Amerigo said, bowing. "How may I serve you?"

"I am naming you Chief Pilot of Spain," the King said. "You will have two responsibilities. You will teach all ships' pilots how to find their way around on the Ocean Sea, and show them your new way of measuring how far east or west they have come by looking at the moon. And you will be in charge of drawing a map of the New World."

"A map?" Amerigo asked.

"Yes." The King nodded. "Any pilot who sails to the new land will be required to visit your home when he returns to Spain, so that you can add his discoveries to the map. Spain will have the best map of the New World! Sailors will come from all over to look at it!"

Amerigo was pleased that the King placed so much trust in him. But part of him was disappointed. Now he could not go on another voyage himself. He would have to be in charge and let others do the exploring.

"I am naming you Chief Pilot of Spain,"
the King said.

Amerigo was Chief Pilot for four years. He did his best to teach the sailors the things they needed to know in order to sail to the new continent, but he was sometimes frustrated by their slowness to learn. He faithfully kept the map of the New World as the King had instructed. Sometimes, alone in his library, he would take out the map and slowly trace his finger along the route he had sailed, remembering the wonderful things he had seen. Sometimes at night, he would lean out the window and stare up at the constellations, and he would see, in his imagination, the strange new stars he had studied while floating along the new world coasts.

He and his wife did not have any children, but Amerigo's nephew, Giovanni, lived with them. Amerigo taught Giovanni just as Uncle Guido had taught him, all those years ago, and eventually Giovanni became Chief Pilot, too, just like his famous uncle.

Amerigo was sick, off and on, during the four years he was Chief Pilot. He had been bitten by a mosquito during his last voyage, and that bite had given him a disease called malaria. In 1512, he became very ill, and in February of that year, he died. Before his death, he truly felt that he had won fame and honor, as he had written in his school notebook so long before.

But even Amerigo would have been amazed by the fame and honor that was to come!

CHAPTER 6

"AMERICA"

High in the mountains of France, a German mapmaker named Martin Waldseemuller was reading a copy of some of Amerigo's letters to the Medici family. These letters had been copied and recopied and passed around, because people were excited at the thought of a new continent. Martin Waldseemuller was excited too. In fact, he was so interested in Amerigo's discoveries that he set aside the map he had been working on, and began instead to draw a new map, a wonderful map showing the three parts of the world, Europe, Africa, Asia. Then, carefully dipping his pen in fresh ink, he drew the outlines of the new continent, the fourth part of the world. He stepped back from his table, pleased with his work, and then realized that the new continent needed a

He set aside the map he had been working on,
and began instead to draw a new map.

name. After a moment's thought, he labeled it AMERICA, in order to give honor to Amerigo Vespucci.

He sent copies of this new map to some of his friends, and they in turn made copies too. Eventually, a lot of people saw that map, or had a copy made for their own library. The name "America" was used by other mapmakers, and sailors going to the New World began telling their friends that they were sailing to "America." After awhile, when a person talked about the New World, he called it America.

What a wonderful way to remember a boy who loved the night sky, who grew up to be a man who loved discovery. Amerigo Vespucci realized that he was looking at a new continent, and we honor him for it every time we say that continent's name.

INDEX

ALSO AVAILABLE FROM PEACE HILL PRESS:

Who in the World Was the UNREADY KING?
THE STORY OF ETHELRED

by Connie Clark
illustrations by Jed Mickle

Ethelred's mother stood behind him. The archbishop smeared holy oil on Ethelred's shoulders and hands. He gave Ethelred a heavy sword and placed a gold crown on his head. The crown was too big—it fell over his eyes, and Ethelred almost dropped the sword on the archbishop's foot. **How did Ethelred become king when he was only ten years old?**

Discover the intriguing story of Ethelred, England's last Anglo-Saxon king. In this engaging biography, Connie Clark tells the tale of the boy king who handed England over to the Vikings. How did Ethelred and his sons lose their country to the northern invaders? Find out, with *Who in the World Was the Unready King? The Story of Ethelred*.

DISTRIBUTED BY W.W. NORTON

ISBN 0-9728603-7-1 $9.50